making smart choices ™

making smart choices about
violence, gangs, and bullying

Matt Monteverde

rosen publishing's
rosen central

New York

For my grandma

Published in 2008 by The Rosen Publishing Group, Inc.
29 East 21st Street, New York, NY 10010

First Edition

Library of Congress Cataloging-in-Publication Data

Monteverde, Matthew.
Making smart choices about violence, gangs, and bullying / Matthew Monteverde.—1st ed.
    p. cm.—(Making smart choices)
Includes bibliographical references and index.
ISBN-13: 978-1-4042-1387-6 (library binding)
1. Violence in adolescence. 2. Juvenile delinquency. 3. Gangs.
4. Bullying in schools. 5. Youth and violence. I. Title.
HQ799.2.V56M66 2008
303.60835—dc22

                                                                    2007031581

Manufactured in Malaysia

contents

introduction

As you go through your teen years, you will be presented with many new challenges. Some may be easy to overcome, and others will be more difficult. With each challenge, whether big or small, comes the responsibility of making choices. Choices regarding violence may be among the most important that you will have to make. Why are they important? Because the choices you make regarding violent behavior are crucial to your own physical well-being, as well as that of others.

Violence is a complex subject. You might

Bullying is the most common form of violence in our society. If you find yourself threatened by a bully, how will you react?

find it difficult to make decisions in a violent situation. In order to make it easier to make choices about violence, it is important to educate yourself on the subject. It helps to understand what violent behavior is, as well as where it occurs and why it occurs. Knowledge of the subject will help you identify the challenges that violence presents. Then, when you have an understanding of violence, you can use your knowledge to make smart decisions.

As a teen, you will probably come across situations that could lead to some sort of violence. For instance, maybe you or someone you know has been invited to join a gang. More likely, maybe you or someone you know is being bullied at school. Factors such as your upbringing, peer pressure, and advice from your parents or a role model could have an influence on the choices that you make. It is important to understand these factors and the way they influence you. Good influences will help you make the best decision and achieve the best results.

chapter one

Teens and Violence

A student attends a candlelight vigil held to remember the victims of the Columbine High School shootings.

Violence occurs in many different forms. Some forms of violence are considered mild. Acts such as yelling, pushing, bullying, and school fights are considered mild forms of violence. Mild acts of violence are usually not considered criminal. They may result in punishments like verbal warnings or detention. In contrast, more serious forms of violence are considered criminal offenses. These include gang violence, weapon violence, vandalism, sexual assault, and dating (sexual) violence. Such acts are usually punishable by jail time.

Teen Violence in the News

Teenagers are typically involved in mild forms of violence, especially bullying. That is not to say that they do not engage in more serious forms of violence. Statistics show that teenage violence has been in sharp decline since the early 1990s. The *New York Times* reported that between 1982 and 1992, violent crime by juveniles in the United States increased more than 25 percent. That means that teenage violence had become alarmingly common during that time. However, according to the *Yale Herald*, as of 2007, juvenile crime has been at a thirty-year low. Although statistics show that crime has become less frequent in the United States, it is still a cause for concern.

One of the most horrific acts of teenage violence occurred on April 20, 1999, at Columbine High School in Jefferson County, Colorado. On that day, two students shot and killed twelve students and a teacher in what has come to be known as the Columbine Massacre. The Columbine shooters were influenced by several factors, including revenge for being victims of harassment and violence at their school.

Factors That Make Teens Choose Violence

Violent behavior is sometimes a preconceived, or planned, act. One may go through a complex thought process prior to deciding whether or not to act violently. On the other hand, something unexpected may happen to trigger a violent response. For example, seeing somebody steal your wallet out of your gym locker is a trigger event. Your first thought might be, "How can I get my wallet back?" You may think that your best chance to get it back would be through immediate intimidation and/or physical violence.

Dating violence is another common form of violence that teenagers may encounter. Jealous or angry boyfriends or girlfriends, especially, are known to commit violent acts. Would you react with violence if your wallet were stolen? Or would you react violently if your boyfriend or girlfriend did something you didn't like? Whether you answer yes or no to these questions depends on several factors. Among the most influential factors are:

- Whether you have experienced abuse at home
- Whether you have role models
- Your exposure to and understanding of violence in the media
- Peer pressure

These aspects of who you are will have an effect on how you view violent behavior. In chapter 3, we'll see different ways of dealing with exposure to violence. We'll also learn what your best options are in case you find yourself in a violent situation.

Abuse at Home

Teenagers don't often wake up one day and decide to live a violent lifestyle. Instead, the roots of their violent behavior can usually be traced back to when they were children. This is especially true if a teen grew up in a violent home. Children who grow up in a home where domestic abuse or other violent acts occur often believe that violence is acceptable, a normal part of life. Some parents even promote threats and violent behavior because they find it is the easiest and best way to solve problems.

Although you do not get to choose who your family is, you do have the right to choose what to do if you are part of a violent household. If you witness domestic abuse or other violence at home, you can turn to an adult, sibling, or peer for help. You can also seek help from a teacher or guidance counselor at school. In situations where you feel seriously threatened, you can even contact the police. If you are living in an abusive home, remember that you are not the only one who has experienced such abuse. Violence at home is a widespread problem. There are trained professionals

It is normal for teens to disagree with their parents. However, abusive or violent behavior is not the best way to settle disputes at home.

who can get people the help they need based on their type of situation. It is important not to isolate yourself or try to overcome an abusive situation by yourself. If you choose to do this, you will make it harder for yourself to work through the problem of violence. Don't be afraid or embarrassed to seek help. Those who are able to give you help can offer you emotional support, which you cannot get by acting by yourself.

Lack of Role Models

A role model is a person, usually an adult, whom a child can look up to for guidance and advice. Children who grow up in a violent home often lack good role models. Lack of guidance from a role model or other adult figure can make it difficult for a child or teenager to make important decisions, including decisions regarding violence.

Young people greatly respect their role models, so much so that children will often make decisions based on what they think their role models would do. For example, let's say that your parents are your role models. If you find yourself in an unfamiliar or unpleasant situation, you might think to yourself, "What would my mom or dad do in this situation?" Or, "What would they want me to do in this type of situation?" Thoughts like these are common for someone who has a role model to look up to. If you have a role model, he or she will influence the decisions you will ultimately make.

When it comes to making choices regarding violence, a child or teen usually needs some type of guidance. This

Don't be afraid to sit down with your role models to ask for guidance. It's likely that they have faced the same challenges you are facing.

guidance can be as basic as someone simply explaining that violent behavior is wrong. Strong, straightforward guidance can have a long-lasting and positive influence. Without a role model to imitate, you might be quite open to the influence of violent behavior, especially in the form of bullying.

Bullying

People who physically or verbally abuse somebody else for their own personal gain are called bullies. The victim of a bully's abuse is called the target. Bullying is the most common form of violence among teenagers. It usually occurs at school. Bullying takes place when a person harasses or intimidates someone, usually someone smaller or weaker than him or her. This behavior can result in physical aggression, such as shoving, slapping, punching, or kicking. Verbal abuse—yelling, insulting, and swearing—is also considered bullying.

Some teens turn to bullying because they do not know how to work out problems without using violence. Usually, the root problem with bullies is that they have low self-esteem, or a low opinion of themselves. Because they don't feel good about themselves, bullies insult and hurt other people to make themselves feel better.

In the school cafeteria, a bully might regularly harass you until you hand over your lunch money. If so, you may grow tired of the bully's abuse and be forced to make a decision on how to put an end to his or her harassment. When you feel it is time to make a choice on how to handle such a violent situation, you will have reached your decision point. Your choice may be dependent on the influence your role model has on you. Or, it may be influenced by how the media has shaped your view on violent behavior. Later in this book, we'll see some of the ways you can respond to a bully.

Violence in the Media

In today's society, exposure to real-world violence is constant. If you watch the news or look through a newspaper, you are almost certain to find several stories about some type of violent behavior. The stories of violence that are told and retold through the news media give us the impression that violent behavior occurs just about everywhere.

Aside from the news media, the entertainment media constantly features violence as well. Media outlets including movies, music, and video games all have been criticized recently for their violent content. You might have played a first-person shooter video game, such as *Doom* for Sony PlayStation. You might also have listened to gangsta rap music by artists such as Tupac Shakur or the Notorious B.I.G.

The popularity of violent video games can lead you to believe that violence is widely accepted—and even fun.

If so, you probably noticed that violence is commonly the central theme of gangsta rap music.

Common sense tells you that violence is not positive behavior. The entertainment industry, however, often paints a different picture. Some say the entertainment business even promotes violence. That is because the entertainment media often glorifies or puts a positive spin on violence. Television shows like *The Sopranos* emphasize the rewards to bullying and acting violently. The rewards might include money, power over others, and the ability of a person to get what he or she wants, when he or she wants it. It is true that violence can sometimes lead to such rewards. If you feel that it's OK to act violently, you need to decide whether the risks associated with violence are worth the price of the rewards.

chapter two

Why Do Teens Choose Violence?

Widespread teenage violence raises the question of why teens are violent. There is no single answer to this question: behind each act of violence lies a different motivation. Some act violently only when with a certain person or group. Others turn to violence to try to solve problems. Still others turn to violence in order to support a drug habit. And then there are those who choose to engage in violence for fun or a quick thrill.

When friends hang out together all the time, they tend to influence each other. This is peer pressure in action.

Peer Pressure

Many teens act certain ways because of peer

pressure, or influence by friends and others who are about the same age. This leads to copycat behavior, which is often harmless. For example, you might decide to buy the same popular pair of Nike sneakers that your friends have. Or, you might style your hair the same way as a classmate to keep up with the current look.

While peer pressure can play a role in influencing harmless decisions, it can also lead you to make dangerous or risky decisions. For example, one of your peers might try to convince you that wielding a knife to rob a local convenience store cashier is a quick and easy way to get money. Or, you might find yourself being persuaded by someone to join a gang. Many teenagers decide to participate in violence like this because they cannot resist the temptation of peer pressure. Giving in to negative (bad) peer pressure can put you in a dangerous situation.

Some young people participate in violence because they get caught up in a herd or mob mentality. When mob mentality takes over, people do things in a group they would never do acting individually. This is a poor and dangerous excuse to participate in any kind of violence. Just because "everyone else is doing it" doesn't mean you have to, too.

Violence and Drugs

Oftentimes, teen violence is linked to illegal drug use. A recent study by the Substance Abuse and Mental Health Services Administration (SAMHSA) backs up this claim. The study showed that people aged twelve to seventeen who used illegal drugs in 2005 were almost twice as likely to have been involved in violent behavior as those who did not use an illegal drug during that year.

Also according to the SAMHSA study, 49.7 percent of the teens who used marijuana in 2005 engaged in violent behavior that year, more than half of those who used inhalants (called "huffing") were violent, and more than 69 percent of the teens who used methamphetamine ("ice" or crystal meth) in 2005 engaged in violent behavior.

Violent behavior and drugs are paired together for two main reasons. First, drug users often use violence to obtain money to support their drug habit. So, a cocaine user could turn to theft or violent robbery as a way to pay for an expensive habit. Second, the physical and psychological effects of drugs can make a person act violently, recklessly, or aggressively. Drugs, both legal and illegal, can distort a person's mind and alter the decision-making process. When high on drugs, one may even act out violently without even realizing it.

Gangs

Gangs are organized groups that control a "turf" (territory), usually by the use of violence against other gangs. Joining a gang is another way that teenagers become involved in violence. Similar to the seedy culture of illegal drug users and dealers, gangs also embrace a violent lifestyle. In fact, many gangs buy and sell drugs to fund their activities.

To maintain their strong social bonds, these California gang members get distinctive tattoos, dress the same, and share the same beliefs on violence.

Gang life may seem glamorous and exciting from the outside, but in reality, it is very bleak and dangerous. Gang members typically reject mainstream rules and laws. Instead, they attempt to achieve their goals through the use of intimidation and violence.

Gang violence is not limited to just fighting with other gangs. Sometimes, gang violence can spill out onto the streets or into schools. In addition, gangs have also been known to inflict violence on innocent people. Performing a violent act against an innocent bystander is a common gang initiation ritual. Other gang initiations involve armed robbery, theft, or getting beaten.

A common misunderstanding about gangs is that they exist only in low-income or urban settings. While gangs do exist in such areas, they are also found in wealthy and suburban communities. Gangs, like violence itself, are not confined by racial and class boundaries. They can form anywhere, especially in environments where there are few social support groups.

With gangs being so dangerous, you might wonder why someone would want to join one. The main reason young people choose to join gangs is because it supplies them with something they want or need. These wants and needs can be either material or psychological. Material items commonly sought out by gang members include money, vehicles, expensive clothes, and weapons. Psychologically, many teenagers join gangs because they want to experience a sense of belonging among their peers. This is especially true of young people who do not have a sense of belonging in their own families.

Violence and Power

As a teen, you probably like the feeling of being in control. Unfortunately, having power over others, especially over people bigger or older than you, is rare when you are a teen. One of the keys of feeling powerful is believing in your own abilities. It's a simple concept, but many teenagers do not believe in their own abilities. Instead,

In the Bronx, New York, a grieving girl writes a message on a makeshift shrine. Her friend, the fifteen-year-old boy in the picture, was shot to death by another teen following an argument.

they think that they will obtain power and respect by carrying a knife or gun.

The decision to carry a gun can have tragic results. The Children's Defense Fund reports that gunshot wounds are the second leading cause of death among young people, after motor vehicle accidents. Gunshot wounds result from both deliberate shootings and from accidents. Most accidental gun deaths occur when a child plays with a gun that he or she finds in his or her home, but accidental deaths also occur in school and other social settings. According to the Web site for Common Sense About Kids and Guns (http://www.kidsandguns.org), more than 2,794 teens were killed in firearm accidents between 1994 and 2003.

Weapons for Self-Protection

Once violence has occurred, whether at home, school, or elsewhere, people get scared and want to protect themselves. In order to calm fears of violence, some teens may decide to carry a weapon for self-protection. For example, someone who is the constant target of a bully might decide to bring a knife to school, hoping to scare away the bully. If you are the target of a bully, you may have considered such an action. Before you make your final decision, though, it is important that you consider other, nonviolent options.

chapter three
Avoiding Violent Situations

What do you do when school lets out? Participating in after-school activities helps many teens steer clear of violent or potentially violent situations.

You may have been asked, "Don't you have anything better to do with your free time?" If you have, the question probably came from an adult who noticed that you were bored. Maybe you don't consider too much free time to be a problem. But it is a reason some teenagers give for why they choose to engage in violent behavior. Imagine not being able to come up with anything better to do than go out and commit acts of violence!

Recently, some forms of violence have become like a sport for some teens. This disturbing trend can be witnessed on the Internet in the form of videos. Some videos show teenagers beating up a homeless person for fun. Other forms of violent aggression, such as brawls, riots, or fights, have also been posted on the Web. Teens who post these videos online are using the Internet as a way to glorify or show off their violent behavior. What they don't realize is that the footage of the fight or beating can easily be used as criminal evidence against them. Getting into a fight is a bad choice; filming the fight is an even worse choice.

Keeping Busy

Acts of youth violence peak around the time kids are getting out of school (3:00 pm), in contrast to adult violence (11:00 pm). If you find yourself with too much idle time when school lets out, it is important to explore ways to stay occupied in positive activities. For example, you can join the drama club or play in a band. Or, if you are more of the athletic type, joining a sports team might be the thing for you. You could even join a dojo to practice martial arts, which would allow you to work off some steam while increasing your self-confidence. Staying busy with such activities will likely decrease the chance that you will participate in negative violent behavior.

Although filling your free time can keep you away from violence, you cannot make yourself totally immune from it. Violent acts are unpredictable by nature. Therefore, you should be aware of ways to counter violent behavior, should you be confronted with it.

How to Counter Violent Behavior

Even if you try to avoid it, you may still run into a violent situation. If you are the victim of violence or the threat of violence, you do not have to respond in kind. When your crucial decision point comes, there are many nonviolent options you can choose. These include walking away from the problem, rationalization, and getting help from others.

Walk Away from the Problem

Sometimes, your best reaction to violence is not to react at all. Some of our most admired leaders understood this

In Lowell, Massachusetts, a robed Buddhist monk teaches young gang members to pray, meditate, and act peacefully.

idea very well. Jesus Christ, for example, taught that to "turn the other cheek" is a better policy than "an eye for an eye." Gandhi, a popular leader in India, led a successful revolution using nonviolent resistance to government attacks. Martin Luther King Jr., an American hero from the civil rights movement, also rejected violence.

If someone threatens you or confronts you with violence, you can choose not to engage your attacker in any way. Leave the room or area where the tension is high. By walking away, you remove the chance that you will get hurt.

You can also choose to avoid potential trouble spots in the first place. If you know that a bully is going to be standing on a certain corner at a certain time, make sure you aren't there at the same time. Putting space between you and a potentially violent situation makes you safer and also gives you more time to think about your options moving forward. More time gives cooler heads a chance to prevail.

Rationalization

If four of your classmates meet you at your bus stop and challenge you to a fight, it might not be so easy to escape. In such a situation, walking away from the problem may not be your smartest choice. Instead, you can try rationalizing with your attackers. This tactic uses calm, reasonable conversation to defuse a potentially violent situation. In other words, you can try to talk sense to someone who wants to hurt you. People don't normally attack someone

When you get worked up, a verbal argument can quickly escalate into something worse. In such cases, the smart choice is to be cool and rational.

who is treating them with dignity and respect. Here are a couple of tips for rationalizing:

- Make sure that your attackers know that you don't want the situation to turn ugly.
- Back up your calm words with nonthreatening behavior.
- Give your attackers every opportunity to get out of the situation without looking weak or feeling humiliated.

Getting Help from Others

Have you ever been roughed up by a bully? Or have you ever been verbally abused by a classmate? If so, you may feel very alone in such threatening situations. It is important to know that you are not alone. There are several places that you can turn to for help. For example, if you find yourself getting bullied at school, you can tell a teacher or guidance counselor about the situation. If there are no adults around, or if you do not feel comfortable talking to one, then you can always turn to a friend or a classmate. And if you feel seriously threatened by violence, as when weapon or gang violence is involved, then it is probably best to seek help from the police. These choices are always there for you.

chapter four

The Outcomes of Choosing Violence

f you have thought about acting out in a violent way, you probably also thought about the possible outcomes of your actions. Maybe the thought of starting a potentially dangerous fight made you decide to be cool. Maybe you plowed ahead and got involved in a violent altercation anyway. What was the result of your actions? When making choices, the expected outcome of your actions is a very important consideration.

Physical injuries are a painful and visible result of violent behavior.

Negative Outcomes of Choosing Violence

Do you want to be a victim of violence? Of

course not—no one does. The negative physical and mental effects of violence are terrible things to deal with. In an extreme case of violence, an injury may even be fatal. However, it is important to remember that it is not only the victims of violence who suffer from ill effects. If you commit violent acts, you suffer negative consequences as well.

Physical Injury

Physical injury is probably the most obvious negative end result of getting involved in violent behavior. Violent situations are harmful to your physical well-being. Say, for example, you choose to fight a classmate because he or she stole your prom date. There is a chance that you will get injured whether you win or lose the fight. Even if you win the fight and walk away free from injury, you are still at risk—a "rematch" is almost certainly in your future.

Unpleasant Life Changes

You can heal from some physical injuries caused by violence, which means they are only temporary problems. But some of the problems caused by violence have longer-lasting effects. When teens participate in violence and other delinquent behavior, they often experience negative changes in other areas of their lives. Such changes include poor academic grades, problems with family and friends, and a lack of interest in things that used to be fun. In addition, it can be worrisome knowing that someone may be "out to get you" in retaliation for a violent assault. Living with that fear can make you anxious and depressed. Also, criminal activity injures your spirit and lowers others' opinion of you. After all, who trusts a bully or violent mugger?

Legal Trouble

There is a well-known saying, "You do the crime, you do the time." This means that if you participate in criminal activity, then you have to be prepared to pay the consequences. Violence is often considered criminal behavior. Even if a form of violence is not criminal, such as light pushing or shoving, it may still be punishable.

Punishments for mild forms of violence include detention, suspension from school, and verbal warnings, among others. In contrast, punishments for more serious acts of violence can be much harsher. The most severe forms of violence have severe legal consequences for the offender. This is an

Legal trouble is a real consequence of opting for violence. Here, police in Illinois handcuff a student who brought a gun into his school.

important consideration if you decide that violence is the way you want to go. You might successfully end the harassment of a bully by beating him up and sending him to the hospital with a broken nose. But the trade-off is that you might get arrested for assault, which could lead to probation and other legal restrictions. In serious cases, you could even be tried as an adult and end up in jail. So before participating in an assault or other serious act of violence, you should ask yourself, "Is it really worth it?"

"Positive" Outcomes of Choosing Violence

As we have seen, violence is generally considered a negative form of behavior, with undesirable outcomes. However, violence would probably not be a problem if it produced only bad results. Some might try to make the case that there are good things that can come out of choosing violence. While this may be true, you have to look at the bigger picture to see violence for what it is. When you step back, you see that using violence is never the preferred means to an end. The following sections show you how some think violence can be seen in a positive light.

Violence as a Way to Bond

Most teens like to fit in, and many go to great lengths to achieve this goal. In fact, some will even turn to violence in order to reach it. While violence is socially unacceptable, it can be a social bonding activity for those who participate in it. This sense of protection and belonging is a common aspect of gang culture. The "us against them" attitude of gang members often ends up in violent confrontations.

Similarly, choosing to be violent may earn you respect in some circles. Guys don't like to be labeled a "sissy" or a "wuss." So, they might see violent activity as a way of getting a reputation of being manly or macho. The problem with this attitude is that it usually ends up with a series of violent confrontations that can only end badly. Rising to the challenge of a bully creates more trouble than it solves. Sometimes, the truly bold and brave choice is to reject violence.

Quick Money

Some people say that crime pays. This can be true, as robbing or mugging people can get you money quickly. However, the drawbacks of robbery include possible physical injury and arrest. Teens who do not have much money may ignore the consequences and decide to use violence

Carrying a weapon can make others fear you. However, fear is not the same as respect. In the long run, weapons complicate problems and make them bigger.

to turn a quick buck. Sooner or later, however, muggers almost always pick on the wrong person or get caught. In the long run, criminal violence will get you in trouble and may even land you in a juvenile detention facility or jail.

Solution to Your Problems

Another perceived positive outcome of violence is that it can be a solution to your personal problems. If a bully harasses you at school, you might attempt to scare him or her away by threatening to use more violence than the bully. For example, lets say that you find yourself bullied each day in the school cafeteria. You decide to bring a knife into school to scare off the bully. It is likely that once the bully knows you have a knife, he or she will stop harassing you. In this case, bringing a weapon to school to scare off a bully might succeed as a short-term solution to your immediate problem.

But the problem isn't solved just yet. The bully may come back the next day with a knife of his or her own, or worse. In this way, your response actually escalated the violence, or made it worse.

Even if the threat of violence gets the bully off your back, it is important to think of the other possible effects of your actions. For example, you could be arrested or expelled from school for carrying a weapon. Of course, you or the bully could also be seriously injured if the situation turns violent. In any case, violence is wrong, even if you are using it to retaliate against a violent act that was committed against you.

chapter five

Living with the Outcomes of Your Choices

This teen is in jail for delivering a punch that killed a fellow student. As part of a plea deal, he talks to teens about living with the consequences of violence.

Making choices about violence is not easy. You might be afraid that you will make wrong or poor choices. Such concerns are understandable, especially for teens who don't face violent situations much. However, it is important not to be paralyzed by the fear of making the wrong move. Everyone makes decisions they regret. Plus, if you make a wrong decision, it can still be helpful to you, as long as you are able to recognize your mistake and admit you were wrong. A good measure of maturity and intelligence is not making the same mistake twice.

The Outcomes of Your Decisions

Choices you make about issues like violent behavior should be taken very seriously. They can have a direct, long-term effect on your life and your future. Your choices regarding violence are important to you, and they can matter to others as well. For example, if there is anyone present with you during a violent situation, then your choices may determine if the person is physically at risk along with you. This is true even if the other person is not directly involved. Innocent bystanders are the unfortunate victims of violence all the time.

If you and your brother are walking home from school, and a bully approaches you, it is important to think about the safety of you and your brother. One way to handle the situation is to walk away from the bully. If you choose to attack the bully instead, then you and your brother will both be at risk of physical injury. The bully could retaliate and attack you and your brother. Or, the bully might choose to attack your brother because he seems like an easier target to attack. In short, when others are involved, it's even more important to think about consequences and make good choices.

Did I Make a Good Choice?

Nobody lives life making the right decisions all the time. In fact, many choices aren't really "right" or "wrong" and are instead "better" or "not as good." Instead of trying never to make a mistake, a more realistic goal is to try to make more good choices than bad ones. In order to reach this goal, you must be able to recognize a good decision (as well as a bad one). You must consider your decisions and the outcomes that followed. When looking back at choices you made regarding a violent situation, ask yourself: Does the problem of violence still exist, or did the violence go away? If the violence did not go away, did I create an even bigger problem for myself?

Solving the Problem of Violence

If you successfully eliminated the problem of violence from a particular situation, then you have made a good decision. Maybe not the best possible decision, but a good one. For example, let's say you bump into someone in the school cafeteria and knock over his lunch tray. He challenges you to a fight. You apologize and choose to rationalize with him, and he sees

Solving the problem of violence takes the efforts of many. In this photo, three concerned teens try to rationalize with a friend to prevent a fight.

that it would be better to avoid fighting. In this scenario, the problem of violence was eliminated. This means that you made a good decision in handling the problem.

If you choose instead to rise to the challenge and fight, your outcome will not be as good. You would not have eliminated the violence in such a situation. Instead, you would have contributed to the problem. You have set yourself up for a potentially dangerous situation that will probably end up with both parties unhappy. The outcome proves that you made the wrong decision.

Reducing the Severity of the Problem

Have you faced a situation in which you felt it was impossible to avoid a violent confrontation? It can be discouraging to feel this way. Sometimes, others are bent on lashing out, and it is impossible to completely eliminate violence from the situation. In such cases, reducing the severity of a problem can be the next best solution. This is especially important if you find yourself in a violent situation where you cannot simply walk away.

It is not always easy to do, but reducing the severity of a violent situation can be a small victory in an otherwise no-win situation. Maybe you can avoid a beating by handing over whatever an attacker wants and running as fast as you can in the other direction. Or, if you are being bullied and you are with others, you can point out that nobody wants to get hurt and ask that the bully leave the others out of it.

Making the Problem Bigger

If you have been in violent situations, you have probably noticed that some situations are harder to deal with than others. In fact, it is quite possible to make a problem bigger or more likely to turn violent than it originally started out. For example, if there is a shoving match between two players in the baseball locker room, and one player decides to attack the other with a bat, then the situation will almost certainly get much worse.

If you are involved in such a violent situation, it is important not to make the situation worse. Even a simple verbal argument can escalate quickly into physical violence. So it is important to try to resolve even the mildest forms of violence. When you look back on a situation in which violence escalated, you can almost always point to a poor choice that allowed it to happen. As the saying goes, "It's easier to put out fires while they are small."

Learning from Your Decisions

When it comes to working your way through potentially violent situations, you should be able to learn from every choice you make. What was the outcome of your choice? Did you eliminate the violence or the threat of violence? Did you at least reduce the violence or threat? Or did you make the problem worse? You can do this regardless of whether or not you made a good or bad choice. If you made a smart decision in a particular situation, then you can assume the same choice may be

These students are sharing what they have learned in a nonviolence program. Working together, friends can help each other reduce or even eliminate problems stemming from violence.

successful should you encounter a similar scenario in the future. In contrast, if you made a wrong decision and suffered bad consequences, then you will know not to make the same choice again.

Sharing Your Smarts with Others

Making good choices is always easier when you have smart, positive role models or people you can turn to for advice. This book points out that you can use your own experience, too, to make smarter decisions. If you have some knowledge of how to handle a violent situation, you can share your good advice with others. Since it is likely that you and your friends will be confronted with some type of violence during your teenage years, it will be helpful if you can rely on each other for advice. Above all, remember that sharing knowledge about violence with each other will make it easier and safer for you and your friends to handle violent situations. That is a good kind of peer pressure that makes everyone better off.

altercation Noisy disagreement or dispute.

assault To attack.

bully One who harasses or threatens someone for his or her own personal gain.

confrontation Face-to-face meeting between two or more people.

consequences Effects or outcomes of an action.

delinquent One who does not act as the law requires.

harass To verbally or physically attack.

initiation ritual Activity that must be performed in order for an individual to be accepted into a group.

intimidate To threaten or make scared.

mob mentality Mind-set in which people acting as a group do things they would never do individually.

preconceived Planned, or thought out in advance.

psychological Related to the mind, as opposed to the body.

retaliate To get back at someone for insult or injury.

role model Someone whose behavior is copied by others.

self-esteem Feelings you have about yourself.

target Victim of a bully's abuse.

turf Territory or area controlled by a gang.

Brady Center to Prevent Handgun Violence
1225 Eye Street NW, Suite 1100
Washington, DC 20005
(202) 898-0792
Web site: http://www.bradycenter.org
The Brady Center works to educate the public about gun
    violence.

The Center for the Prevention of School Violence
1801 Mail Service Center
Raleigh, NC 27699-1801
(800) 299-6054
Web site: http://www.ncdjjdp.org/cpsv
Established in 1993, the Center for the Prevention of
    School Violence promotes safer schools and positive
    youth development.

National Crime Prevention Council (NCPC)
1000 Connecticut Avenue NW, Thirteenth Floor
Washington, DC 20036
(202) 466-6272
Web site: http://www.ncpc.org

The goal of the NCPC is to keep families and communities
safe from crime. To achieve its goal, the NCPC pro-
duces literature and offers programs that teach crime
prevention techniques.

National Youth Violence Prevention Resource Center
P.O. Box 10809
Rockville, MD 20849-0809
(866) 723-3968
Web site: http://www.safeyouth.org
The Resource Center offers tools to encourage discussion
with children, to resolve conflicts nonviolently, to stop
bullying, and to end violence committed by and
against young people.

Stop Bullying Now!
E-mail: comments@hrsa.gov
Web site: http://stopbullyingnow.hrsa.gov/index.asp
Stop Bullying Now! helps kids and adults understand what
bullying is and how to put a stop to it.

Web Sites

Due to the changing nature of Internet links, Rosen
Publishing has developed an online list of Web sites
related to the subject of this book. This site is updated
regularly. Please use this link to access the list:

http://www.rosenlinks.com/msc/avgb

for further reading

Brown, Brooks, and Rob Merritt. *No Easy Answers: The Truth Behind Death at Columbine.* New York, NY: Lantern Books, 2002.

Coloroso, Barbara. *The Bully, the Bullied, and the Bystander: From Preschool to High School—How Parents and Teachers Can Help Break the Cycle of Violence.* New York, NY: HarperCollins, 2004.

Garbarino, James, and Ellen Dellara. *And Words Can Hurt Forever: How to Protect Adolescents from Bullying, Harassment, and Emotional Violence.* New York, NY: Simon & Schuster, 2003.

Guerra, Nancy G., Ann Moore, and Ronald G. Slaby. *A Guide to Conflict Resolution and Decision Making for Adolescents.* Champaign, IL: Research Press, 1995.

Levy, Barrie. *A Teen's Guide to Breaking Free of Abusive Relationships.* Emeryville, CA: Avalon Publishing Group, Inc., 2006.

Thomas, R. Murray. *Violence in America's Schools: Understanding, Prevention, and Responses.* Westport, CT: Greenwood Publishing Group, Inc., 2006.

White, Katherine. *Everything You Need to Know About Relationship Violence.* New York, NY: Rosen Publishing Group, Inc., 2001.

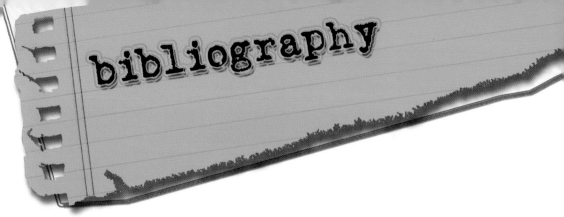

bibliography

Coloroso, Barbara. *The Bully, the Bullied, and the Bystander: From Preschool to High School—How Parents and Teachers Can Help Break the Cycle of Violence.* New York, NY: HarperCollins, 2004.

De Becker, Gavin. *The Gift of Fear: Survival Signals That Protect Us from Violence.* New York, NY: Dell Publishing, 1999.

Focus Adolescent Services. "Violence Leads to Violence." 2000. Retrieved May 18, 2007 (http://www.focusas.com/Violence.html).

Focus Adolescent Services. "Why Do Young People Join Gangs?" 2000. Retrieved May 18, 2007 (http://www.focusas.com/Gangs.html).

Garbarino, James, and Ellen Dellara. *And Words Can Hurt Forever: How to Protect Adolescents from Bullying, Harassment, and Emotional Violence.* New York, NY: Simon & Schuster, 2003.

A Guide to Psychology and Its Practice. "Adolescent Violence." 2007. Retrieved June 1, 2007 (http://www.guidetopsychology.com/ad_viol.htm).

Hardy, Kenneth V., and Tracey A. Laszloffy. *Clinical Interventions to Break the Cycle of Adolescent Violence.* New York, NY: Guilford, 2005.

Horn, Sam. *Take the Bully by the Horns: Stop Unethical, Uncooperative, or Unpleasant People from Running and Ruining Your Life.* New York, NY: St. Martin's Press, 2003.

Horn, Sam. *Tongue Fu! How to Deflect, Disarm, & Defuse Any Verbal Conflict.* New York, NY: St. Martin's Press, 1996.

Jackson, Robert K., and Wesley D. McBride. *Understanding Street Gangs.* Belmont, CA: Wadsworth Publishing, 2000.

Parent Teacher Association. "Safeguarding Your Children from Bullying, Gangs, and Sexual Harassment." 2007. Retrieved June 7, 2007 (http://www.pta.org/pr_magazine_article_details_1117638753468.html).

Spergel, Irving A. *Youth Gang Problem: A Community Approach.* New York, NY: Oxford University Press, 1995.

University of Washington News and Information. "Seattle Gang Study Shows Small Minority of Teens Responsible for More Than Half of Adolescent Crime." 1996. Retrieved May 24, 2007 (http://uwnews.washington.edu/ni/article.asp?articleID=3058).

index

About the Author

Matt Monteverde is a writer currently living in Summit, New Jersey. He earned a bachelor's degree in sociology from Rutgers University in 2003.

Photo Credits

Cover Shutterstock.com; pp. 4, 9 © Topham/The Image Works; pp. 6, 13, 24 © Getty Images; p. 11 © David Young-Wolff/Photo Edit; p. 15 © www.istockphoto.com/ericsphotography; p. 18 © A. Ramey/Photo Edit; p. 20 © Monika Graf/The Image Works; p. 22 © David Grossman/The Image Works; p. 26 © Richard Lord/The Image Works; p. 28 © www.istockphoto.com/Pattie Steib; p. 30 © Journal-Courier/The Image Works; p. 32 © www.istockphoto.com/Daniel Silva; p. 34 © AP Images; p. 36 © Bob Daemmrich/The Image Works; p. 39 © Jeff Greenberg/The Image Works.

Designer: Tahara Anderson; **Editor:** Christopher Roberts